IDENTIFIED WITH CHRIST

IDENTIFIED WITH CHRIST

A COMPLETE CYCLE
FROM DEFEAT TO VICTORY

by

Frederick K.C. Price, Ph.D.

FAITH ONE
PUBLISHING
LOS ANGELES, CALIFORNIA

Unless otherwise indicated, all Scripture quotations are taken from the *King James Version* of the Bible.

Identified With Christ: A Complete Cycle From Defeat to Victory
ISBN 1-883798-11-6
Copyright © 1995 by
Frederick K.C. Price, Ph.D.
P.O. Box 90000
Los Angeles, CA 90009

Published by Faith One Publishing
7901 South Vermont Avenue
Los Angeles, California 90044

CONTENTS

Introduction

Being a Christian is more than having a good emotional feeling, trying to live on that feeling, and going on to heaven after you physically die. Christianity is a way of life. It is a life that can be productive, joyous, and beautiful. It is a life that can exemplify to the world a very beautiful image of the Lord Jesus Christ as people see Christ in us as the **"hope of glory."** In short, Christianity is living the God kind or God quality of life.

For us to live this God kind of life, we must understand who we are, what we are, and where we are in Christ Jesus. We need to understand what makes us the children of God — and by that, I mean more than the fact of accepting Christ as our personal Savior, and confessing Him as the Lord of our lives. There are certain legal transactions that have taken place in the realm of the spirit — in the realm of God — which make us a part of the family of God, and we need to know that.

We also need to appreciate what we are, relative to the Father God and the Lord Jesus Christ. We need to learn how God sees us, how He evaluates us, and looks at us as His children. We need this because it is a foundational truth; and when we understand this truth, it will give us a better grasp of what it means to be a child of God. Once we learn to see ourselves as God sees us, it will help us tremendously in living the overcoming Christian life.

To understand and appreciate all this, we are going to talk about *identification*. It is a very beautiful subject, one in which every Christian should be rooted and grounded. In fact, it may be the most important subject you will ever read or study. As you follow along, you will be able to see how important the word *identification* really is.

Many people live on the very shallow, ragged edge of being a Christian, in terms of the manifestation of the Christ kind of life. This is simply because they do not know who they are in Christ.

Many times, these people have been conditioned by theology, tradition and denominationalism to think of themselves as not being worth very much. They think of themselves as "old sinners saved by grace," unworthy of the blessings of God. It is a downplaying of themselves in the guise of expressing humility.

That is not how God sees us!

When you live with this attitude, and say, "Oh, I don't know why God is blessing me, because I'm so unworthy," it is really an insult to the intelligence of Almighty God. God may be blessing you because you deserve to be blessed. Did you ever think of that?

The Father God treats us and everything relative to our relationship with Him in the same way He treats Jesus. He deals with us through Jesus, and anything He did for Jesus, He will do for us. This is because we are identified with Christ in our relationship with God and in the privileges we can enjoy as children of God.

Therefore, knowing how we are identified with Christ is crucial.

Once you learn to see yourself as identified with Christ, it will elevate your sights in terms of how you view yourself. Instead of seeing yourself as just an "old sinner saved by grace," or as someone not worth very much, you will have the estimate of yourself that the Father has of you.

God's estimate of us is a very high and exalted one. Once that appraisal takes root in your spirit, you will not consider yourself second best.

1

What Is Identification?

Before we start discussing identification, we need to qualify our words. Words can mean different things to different people. They can have different shadings of meaning or different connotations to different individuals. If you do not know what I mean, I will only confuse you, and confusion is not the name of the game here. Understanding and revelation are what we are after.

According to Webster's Dictionary, *identify* means "to cause to be or become identical; to conceive as united (as in spirit, outlook, or principle); ... to be or become the same." For instance, when someone has become identified with the civil rights movement or the labor movement, you associate him or her with that movement. When you think of that movement, you think of that person, and vice versa.

In other words, *identification* means "the condition or fact of being the same in all qualities under consideration." It means "sameness or oneness."

Christ, Our Substitute

When Jesus ascended to heaven after the Resurrection and offered His divine blood as a sacrifice for the sin of Adam (and thus the sin of all mankind), He obtained for us eternal redemption. He did this on the basis of His substitutionary death and resurrection on our behalf. He came to this world for the specific purpose of redeeming us and bringing us into right relationship with the Father God, so everything Jesus did was done for our benefit.

Because Jesus was, in effect, our substitute, we became participants with Him, and God sees us identified with Jesus. We are associated in the mind and sight of God with Jesus, so whatever Jesus did, God accounts it as though we did it. When Jesus died, we died. When Jesus rose, we rose. When Jesus defeated Satan, we defeated Satan.

Hebrews 9:11-12:

But Christ being come an high priest of good things to come, by a greater and more perfect tabernacle, not made with hands, that is to say, not of this building;

Neither by the blood of goats and calves, but by his own blood he entered in once into the holy place, having obtained eternal redemption for us.

We could read these verses like this: "But Christ being come an high priest of good things to come, by a greater and more perfect tabernacle, not made with hands, that is to say, not of this building; neither by the blood of goats and calves, but by Christ's own blood, Christ entered in once into the holy place, having obtained eternal redemption for [your name]."

Notice, it does not say Jesus obtained eternal redemption for Himself. He did it for us. We are the ones who are the recipients of what He did.

Hebrews 10:5-14:

> Wherefore when he [Jesus] cometh into the world, he saith, Sacrifice and offering thou wouldest not, but a body hast thou prepared me:
>
> In burnt offerings and sacrifices for sin thou hast had no pleasure.
>
> Then said I, Lo, I come (in the volume of the book it is written of me,) to do thy will, O God.
>
> Above when he said, Sacrifice and offering and burnt offerings and offering for sin thou wouldest not, neither hadst pleasure therein; which are offered by the law;
>
> Then said he, Lo, I come to do thy will, O God. He taketh away the first, that he may establish the second.
>
> By the which will we [and here you should insert your name] are sanctified through the offering of the body of Jesus Christ once for all.
>
> And every priest standeth daily ministering and offering oftentimes the same sacrifices, which can never take away sins:
>
> But this man, after he had offered one sacrifice for sins for ever, sat down on the right hand of God;
>
> From henceforth expecting till his enemies be made his footstool.
>
> For by one offering he hath perfected for ever them that are sanctified.

We just read in verse 10,

... by the which will we are sanctified.

We are sanctified refers to the same sanctified people mentioned in verse 14: **For by one offering he hath perfected for ever them that are sanctified.**

Notice this: Jesus did what is described in these verses, but He did it on our behalf. Because of this, God counts it as though we did it. When Christ sat down at the right hand of the Father, mankind had been perfectly redeemed, because mankind had been legally identified with Christ in His redemptive work.

Identified With Sin

You need to realize that man's spiritual death was due to the fact that mankind had been legally identified with Adam. Adam was the first man God created. That made Adam mankind's representative. Every person who came after Adam inherited his spiritual condition, because everything he did legally affected us, just the same as when world leaders and other representatives of government make decisions that affect our society.

That also means we have to pay the price for whatever our representative does, good or bad. When Adam sinned and disobeyed God, every one of his children had to reap the same whirlwind. That is why every man is a sinner before he accepts Christ as his personal Savior and Lord.

Some people may say, "I don't think it is fair that everyone is born in sin and conceived in iniquity." But wait a minute! You could say that if God had not given us a way out of sin. If God had left us as victims of the circumstances with no escape whatsoever, then we could say God is unjust to consider us as sinners and to send us to hell when we physically die.

God did not do that, however. John 3:16 says, **For God so loved the world, that he gave his only begotten Son, that whosoever believeth in him should not perish, but have everlasting life.** He sent Jesus to undo what Adam had done and to give everyone an opportunity to receive right-standing with Him.

The beautiful part about God sending Jesus is that it gives us an opportunity to know whether or not we would have done the same thing Adam did when Adam was in the Garden of Eden. Many people say, "If I had been Adam, I never would have messed up like that." Hindsight is always better than foresight.

God gives you the opportunity to accept His Son by faith, and to receive Him as your personal Savior. You had nothing to do with Adam's sinning, but now you have a choice. What are you going to do? **For God so loved the world, that he gave his only begotten Son, that whosoever....** *Whosoever* includes you. If you say, "I'm not going to accept Jesus," you would have blown it in the Garden just as Adam did.

When we were identified with Adam, it was sin. When we are identified with Jesus, it is redemption. God has turned the tables and given us a way out. We had no choice about being born with a sin nature, but it is our fault if we die with that nature and go to hell. You can be identified with Jesus, and it will absolutely undo what Adam did.

What Salvation Really Is

Most Christians truly do not realize what salvation and redemption are all about. They think it is just "church" or "religion," and treat it as though it were a picnic. They dress up on Sunday, go to church, act nice, sing a few songs, and say, "Hallelujah! Praise the Lord!" Then they act selfish and ugly the rest of the week.

These people feel that salvation and redemption are nothing big. They feel it has nothing to do with their life-style, how successful they are in life, or whether or not their kids go to college. That is where they make a grave mistake.

Redemption and salvation mean every aspect of your life revolves around your relationship with Jesus Christ. When you understand that, and begin to truly appreciate it, you will be able to live your life with vim, vigor, and vitality, because you will really understand what your life is all about.

2

Crucified and Dead
With Christ

There are six steps in our identification with Christ. I will refer to each of these steps in the first person, and I want you to think of them as referring only to yourself — not to the preacher, the person down the street, or the person at the other side of the room. This is because I want you to take them and use them for yourself. Yes, these steps refer to every Christian, and yes, we are all part of the collective body known as the Body of Christ. However, identification with Christ — as well as the Christian experience in general — begins on a very personal level, with you and the Lord.

Step One — I Was Crucified With Christ

The first of the six steps is, **I was crucified with Christ**. The Apostle Paul mentions this point in Galatians 2:20:

> I am crucified with Christ: nevertheless I live; yet not I, but Christ liveth in me: and the life which I now live in the flesh I live by the faith of the Son of God, who loved me, and gave himself for me.

What does Paul mean, **I am crucified with Christ?** Paul was not at Calvary when Jesus was crucified. He was not hanging on the cross. If we use what Paul says here for ourselves — and this is what we are supposed to do — what does he mean?

Paul can say "I was crucified with Christ" because this is the way God sees the Christian. When Christ was crucified, He was not crucified for Himself, or for anything He had done. He was crucified for us. Therefore, when God saw Jesus crucified, He actually, literally saw you, me, and every other Christian on that cross. Nails were driven into our hands. A spear was thrust in our sides. Christ was the one actually experiencing these wounds, but we get the benefits of all that He went through.

Romans 4:25:

Who was delivered for our offences, and was raised again for our justification.

You could and should put your name in the place of "our" in this verse. It is talking about us — me and you — and you need to see yourself in the way this verse describes you. Jesus was delivered for your offenses. He was raised again for your justification.

2 Corinthians 5:20-21:

Now then we are ambassadors for Christ, as though God did beseech you by us: we pray you in Christ's stead, be ye reconciled to God.

For he [God] hath made him [Christ] to be sin for us, who knew no sin; that we might be made the righteousness of God in him.

Again, put your name in place of "we" and "us." We are the righteousness of God in Christ. Jesus did this for us.

What more can a man do to show that he loves you than to die for you? Some people think, "Nobody cares for me. I'm so lonely. I'm so forlorn. God doesn't even care about me." That is not true. Here is a man who died for you, who took your penalty of sin and everything connected with it that belonged to you, and let you go free — and He did it all for you.

There is no greater love than that. Jesus Himself says in John 15:13, **Greater love hath no man than this, that a man lay down his life for his friends.** He then adds in verse 14, **Ye are my friends, if** — *if* is the qualifier here — **ye do whatsoever I command you.**

Step Two — I Died With Christ

The second step in looking at ourselves as identified with Christ is, **I died with Christ.** You may say, "Well, Brother Price, I don't understand that. It would seem that, if I were crucified, I would have died." That is not necessarily the case.

Crucifixion was a very slow, agonizing form of capital punishment. People hanged on crosses sometimes for days before they died, and their entire bodies and minds were affected by it. Sometimes the governor would pardon a criminal who had been crucified, and the criminal would be taken down from the cross while he was still alive. He would perhaps be an invalid as a result of what he had gone through, but at least he would be alive. Being crucified, therefore, did not necessarily mean you were going to die.

Spiritual Death, Then Physical Death

We are going to tread on some very heavy spiritual ground in the following paragraphs. In fact, when you read some of these things I am about to expound on, they may be so far afield in terms of what you may have been exposed to in your church that you may be tempted to say, "I can't accept that. That can't be right."

However, all I will ask you to do is to be fair enough to examine what I say in total before you make a value judgment. Do not reject it simply because it sounds different from what you may have been taught before, but go back through the Word of God, meditate on it, and weigh it for yourself. The Word should be your final authority on what is spiritually right — not your denomination, not your preacher, and certainly not me.

Paul writes in Romans 6:5 and 8,

> **For if we have been planted together in the likeness of his death, we shall be also in the likeness of his resurrection:....**
> **Now if we be dead with Christ, we believe that we shall also live with him.**

Paul did not put a period after, ... **if we be dead.** He wrote, ... **if we be dead with Christ.** When the Bible says Jesus **bowed his head, and he gave up the ghost,** meaning that He physically died, God saw you die, also.

Here is something that may take a while to settle in your mind. Jesus had to die twice. He had to die spiritually before He could die physically, because physical death is actually the child of its parent, spiritual death. Let me give you some evidence from the Word to prove my point.

In the story of Adam and Eve in the Garden of Eden, God said to Adam, **Of every tree of the garden thou mayest freely eat: But of the tree of the knowledge of good and evil, thou shalt not eat of it: for in the day that thou eatest thereof thou shalt surely die** (Gen. 2:16-17). God did not say there was a 60-40 chance Adam would die. He said, **Thou shalt surely die.**

Eve ate of the tree of the knowledge of good and evil, then Adam ate of it, but they did not physically die. However, if you are very spiritual, you will notice that when they ate, **the eyes of them both were opened, and they knew that they were naked; and they sewed fig leaves together, and made themselves aprons** (Gen. 3:7).

Their physical eyes already had to be open for them to know which trees to eat from and not to eat from. This verse is talking about the eyes of their self-consciousness.

When Adam was created, he was God-conscious, not self-conscious. That was why he and Eve could walk around the Garden stark naked with no problems.

Because they were God-conscious, they were operating out of their highest nature, their spiritual nature, so physical things were really irrelevant and immaterial to them.

Notice also that when the eyes of their self-consciousness were opened, Adam and Eve *knew* they were naked. They did not begin seeing it at that moment. They had already seen it. However, they now knew it from the standpoint of self-consciousness. Immediately, because they now had guilt and sin-consciousness, they saw being naked as something negative, and knew they had to cover up.

The moment the Bible says their eyes were opened is actually when Adam and Eve died spiritually. They instantly died spiritually, and slowly began to die physically. We can see, then, that physical death is a by-product of spiritual death.

Spiritually Innocent, Not Spiritually Perfect

Adam was created without sin. He had a spiritual nature that was perfectly innocent, but that nature was not perfect. He was perfect, flawless, physically speaking. Every limb, organ, and cell functioned exactly as God designed them to function. However, Adam was not created morally or spiritually perfect, in the sense of being total or complete.

By virtue of his obedience to the command of God, Adam could have moved from moral and spiritual innocence to moral and spiritual perfection by an act of his own will. Adam had everything going for him when it came to doing that. He had no reason to fail, because he did not have the tug of past generations of sin in his genealogy to force him or lead him into sin. But not sinning was Adam's choice.

That was why God told Adam not to eat of the tree of the knowledge of good and evil — to give his will something to act on. If you do not have any choice, there is nothing to prove you are what you say you are. You cannot say you are too honest to steal until you have been given the opportunity to steal and get away with it. You cannot say you would not cheat on your spouse unless you have had the chance to prove you would not do it.

For God to redeem man, another man like Adam had to come on the scene, and stand in the same position Adam was in before he sinned. The man had to be morally and spiritually innocent, like Adam was, and be given the same opportunity to obey or disobey God. The actions of this man would either bring mankind back into right relationship with God, or confirm the condition mankind was already in.

That man was Jesus Christ, and the fact that He had to be spiritually innocent was the reason for the virgin birth. By coming into the world as He did, Jesus bypassed the normal passage of generation. If Joseph had been Jesus' father, Jesus would have inherited Joseph's sin nature. He would have been in need of a savior Himself, and would not have been able to save anyone else.

For this reason, God bypassed Joseph and had Mary impregnated by the power of the Holy Spirit. Jesus received a physical body from Mary, in which His spirit and soul could function in this physical realm, but

His nature came directly from God, not from Joseph. Because God did this, Jesus received a spiritually innocent nature, like Adam's was before he sinned, and He became "the last Adam" (1 Cor. 15:45) for all mankind.

Moving Into Spiritual Perfection

Jesus came and lived 33½ years, but it was only during the last three and a half years that He actually had a public ministry and acted on our behalf as our representative. During those three and a half years, He showed us conclusively that a person could live in this world without sin and obey the Word of God.

Most of us have copped out with the idea, "Well, everyone sins. We're just sinners, and we do not know any better." That is an erroneous statement. The Bible says in Hebrews 4:15 that Jesus **was in all points tempted like as we are, yet without sin.** He had to be able to sin, or else He could never be tempted in all points like as we are.

Matthew 4:1-3:
> **Then was Jesus led up of the spirit into the wilderness to be tempted of the devil.**
> **And when he had fasted forty days and forty nights, he was afterward an hungred.**
> **And when the tempter came to him....**

Why would the devil waste his time tempting Jesus if he knew Jesus could not yield to the temptation? Granted, the devil is stupid, but he is not that stupid.

What would be the purpose of the devil tempting Jesus? What would be the end result he would be after? To get Jesus to yield to temptation — in short, to sin.

Matthew 4:8-10:

> Again, the devil taketh him up into an exceeding high mountain, and sheweth him all the kingdoms of the world, and the glory of them;
> And saith unto him, All these things will I give thee, if thou wilt fall down and worship me.
> Then saith Jesus unto him, Get thee hence, Satan: for it is written, Thou shalt worship the Lord thy God, and him only shalt thou serve.

Notice what the devil offered Jesus, and notice that Jesus did not say, "Devil, you know you are lying. You can't give me all the kingdoms of the world." Jesus knew the devil could do that. Otherwise, the devil's offering Him all the kingdoms of the world would not have been a temptation to Him. It is like someone offering me a million dollars to get pregnant. That would not be a temptation for me, even if I wanted the money, because I cannot get pregnant. For any woman, however, that could be a temptation.

The beautiful part is that He did not yield to temptation. Instead, He countered the devil with the Word of God. That is what we also should do.

First Peter 2:21 says, **For even hereunto were ye called: because Christ also suffered for us, leaving us an example, that ye should follow his steps.** Jesus is our example. He did not yield to the temptations that came to Him. That means you do not have to yield to them, either. You cannot say, "I couldn't help myself," because Jesus showed us that we can help ourselves.

Dying Twice

As I said earlier in this chapter, for Jesus to redeem us, and for Romans 6:8 to be true, He had to die twice — spiritually first, then physically — because physical death is the direct result of spiritual death. If there had been no spiritual death, there could be no physical death. Jesus did not have a sin nature, so physical death had no claim on Him.

I would not be dogmatic about what I am about to say. I would not argue with you about the exact time, hour, and day it happened, but somewhere between Jesus' praying in the garden of Gethsemane and the cross, Jesus died spiritually. Personally, I believe it was when He was in the garden, when He said, **O my Father, if it be possible, let this cup pass from me: nevertheless not as I will, but as thou wilt** (Matt. 26:39). The cup was a symbol that represented all of the dregs of sin, and all that is associated with it, and Jesus had to drink from that cup.

The reason Jesus was praying in the garden was that His nature — His spirit and soul — were rebelling against the idea of becoming tainted with sin. He was not rebelling against the will of God, because Jesus was not in opposition to doing the will of God, but His spirit and soul had never been separated from God.

Spiritual death means separation from God. That means you are cut off from God, and you have no fellowship or communion with Him. Jesus had always enjoyed sweet, beautiful communion with the Father. In essence, Jesus' spirit rose up on the inside of him and said, "Do I have to do this? Isn't there another way?"

That was why, as the Bible tells us, Jesus prayed in agony. In fact, he prayed to the extent that He actually sweated blood out of His pores. His spirit cried out against having to become separated from the Father in spiritual death, but He submitted Himself to the will of God for you and for me.

Three Days in Hell

What redeemed us, spiritually speaking, was not Jesus' being nailed to the cross. Many people think being nailed to the cross was the punishment for Adam's sin, but it was not. It was simply the door through which Jesus' spirit and soul could leave His body.

Remember, you are a spirit. You have a soul, and you live in a physical body. What you see in the mirror when you look at yourself is not the real you, but simply the house you live in. The real you is a spirit that resides inside your physical body.

The spirit and the soul never die in the sense that they cease to exist. Even when you are what the Bible calls spiritually dead, it does not mean your spirit and soul are nonexistent. You will always be alive as a spirit, either in the presence of God or in the lake of fire, and the Bible confirms that. However, the only way your spirit and soul can permanantly leave your physical body is through physical death.

Spiritual death put Jesus in position to die physically at Calvary. When Jesus said, **Father, into thy hands I commend my spirit** (Luke 23:46), the Bible says He bowed His head and **gave up the ghost** — meaning that He let death come so His spirit and soul could leave.

The moment Jesus bowed His head, His spirit and soul rushed out of His body and went into the ground to the center of the earth, to the place commonly called "hell." In the Bible, it is referred to as the underworld, and it was divided into two parts. One part was paradise, and the other part was called "hell" or, rightfully, "hades." Jesus' spirit and soul went into hades, and stayed there three days and three nights, serving the sentence meant for us.

Let me show you something to back this up, because some would say, "Brother Price, I can't accept that. Jesus in hell — that's sacrilegious! That's heresy! That's false doctrine!"

That is also what the Bible says He did. In the second chapter of Acts, after the Holy Spirit had come upon the 120 disciples in the upper room on the day of Pentecost, the Apostle Peter made this statement. Read it very carefully.

Acts 2:22-27:

Ye men of Israel, hear these words; Jesus of Nazareth, a man approved of God among you by miracles and wonders and signs, which God did by him in the midst of you, as ye yourselves also know:

Him, being delivered by the determinate counsel and foreknowledge of God, ye have taken, and by wicked hands have crucified and slain:

Whom God hath raised up, having loosed the pains of death: because it was not possible that he should be holden of it.

For David speaketh concerning him, I foresaw the Lord always before my face, for he is on my right hand, that I should not be moved:

Therefore did my heart rejoice, and my tongue was glad; moreover also my flesh shall rest in hope:

Because thou wilt not leave my soul in hell, neither wilt thou suffer thine Holy One to see corruption.

The word *hell* in verse 27, in the original Greek, is the word *hades.* Jesus' spirit and soul were not in the garden tomb. His body was there, but His spirit and soul were in the hades section of the underworld.

But Wasn't Jesus in Paradise?

On the cross, Jesus said something very striking. He actually made seven statements, but one of them is very important for us to understand relative to what we are talking about.

Luke 23:39-43:

And one of the malefactors which were hanged railed on him, saying, If thou be Christ, save thyself and us.

But the other answering rebuked him, saying, Dost not thou fear God, seeing thou art in the same condemnation?

And we indeed justly; for we receive the due reward of our deeds: but this man hath done nothing amiss.

> **And he said unto Jesus, Lord, remember me**
> **when thou comest into thy kingdom.**
> **And Jesus said unto him, Verily I say unto thee,**
> **to day shalt thou be with me in paradise.**

This is from the King James Bible, and you may have a Bible that phrases these verses of scripture similarly. Unfortunately, the punctuation marks in the Bible were not divinely inspired. They were not in the original texts, but were added by the translators. Therefore, sometimes the punctuation is not quite what it ought to be and leaves the wrong impression about these verses.

According to the King James, Jesus says in Luke 23:43, **... Verily I say unto thee, to day shalt thou be with me in paradise.** However, Jesus was not going to be in paradise that day. He was going to hell. We just read in Acts 2:27 that God was not going to leave Jesus' spirit and soul in hell. Paradise is not hell, and hell is not paradise. There is a difference.

Let me quote Luke 23:43 from Rotherham's translation, and show you how this verse should read.

> **... I say unto thee this day, with me shalt thou be**
> **in paradise.**

Jesus is saying, "I'm making a statement to you this day. I want everyone to know it for time and eternity. I say unto you this day, with me thou shalt be in paradise." That is a future-tense statement.

Jesus was saying there was a time coming when this thief would be with Him in paradise, because the thief acknowledged Jesus as Lord while he was on the cross, and God received him at that moment. When the thief died, his spirit and soul went to paradise. However, the time Jesus was going to be with the thief in paradise was not the day Jesus died, because the day Jesus died, He did not go into paradise. He went into hell, because He had to serve our sentence first.

After that sentence had been served, Jesus went from hell to paradise and took all the Old Testament saints and the thief out of paradise up to heaven. That is what Paul refers to in Ephesians 4:8 when he says Jesus "led captivity captive, and gave gifts unto men." Every one of those people in paradise went to heaven with Jesus, and as a result of what He did, we were set free.

3
Buried With Christ

Romans 6:1-4:

> What shall we say then? Shall we continue in sin, that grace may abound?
>
> God forbid. How shall we, that are dead to sin, live any longer therein?
>
> Know ye not, that so many of us as were baptized into Jesus Christ were baptized into his death?
>
> Therefore are we buried with him....

When they took Jesus down from the cross, you were not there. When Joseph of Arimathaea and Nicodemus came and took the body of Jesus, wrapped it in a linen cloth and put it in Joseph's brand-new tomb, you were not there, were you? No, not physically.

Look at what the Bible says, however. **Therefore are we buried with him....** We were not there, but God saw us there. God saw us buried with Christ. God saw us go into the garden tomb. That is the third step in our identification with Christ — **I was buried with Christ.**

Notice how Romans 6:4 says we are identified with the death of Christ:

> Therefore are we buried with him by baptism into death....

Water baptism is symbolic of our burial with Christ. However, it is also something that has been very controversial in the Body of Christ. Many people are hung up on the idea that water baptism saves you. Some of those people will be frank enough to tell you that if you are not baptized in water, you are not saved.

Other people will tell you that if you have not been baptized in Jesus' name, you are not saved. Still more will say that if you have not been baptized in the name of the Father, and of the Son, and of the Holy Ghost, you are not saved. Others say that if you are not sprinkled, you are not saved. Some people will also say that if you have not been poured, you are not saved, and others will say that if you have not been immersed, you are not saved. The list is a lengthy one.

Again, water baptism is a symbol of our identification with Jesus. It is a symbol of the fact that when Jesus was buried, we were buried with Him.

Colossians 2:12:
> **Buried with him in baptism....**

Romans 6:4 and Colossians 2:12 very clearly tell us how God sees us. **Buried with him** [Christ].... How? **In** [or by] **baptism....**

What Form Of Water Baptism?

What I am about to say may irritate some people, but I have researched it, and I have taken the time to find out about it. If you do not agree with me, that is fine. Let us not fall out over it, but what I have to say connects directly with, "Buried with him in baptism...."

Let me start by asking you a question. When a person dies physically, and the funeral, eulogy, or memorial service is over, what do they do with the body? Do they take the body out of the casket and throw it out in the middle of the local freeway? No. They usually either cremate or bury the body.

What constitutes burial? What does burial indicate? When you say you bury something, you submerge it or cover it up. You can put the deceased's coffin in a mausoleum, a crypt, or in the ground. In any case, the coffin is covered over and protected from the outside atmosphere.

Think about what we just read in Romans and Colossians about baptism as a symbol of our being buried with Christ. Again, I am not trying to get on anyone's denominational case, but if you bury a dead body, do you sprinkle some dirt on the body and walk away? No. Do you pour a little bit of dirt on the dead person's head and walk away? No.

The only method that can adequately be the end result of the purpose of burial is immersion — not because immersion may be a method used by a certain church or denomination, but because baptism is really a type of burial — an immersion.

The words *baptism* and *baptize* come from the Greek word *baptizo*, which means "to dip into, submerge, or immerse." A good illustration of this is when you wash your dishes by hand. Usually, you put the dirty dishes in a sink or pan full of water, clean each piece with your dishcloth or whatever else you may use, and then rinse it off. The point is, the dirty dishes are usually completely covered with water when you put them into the sink or pan.

That is literally what the word *baptizo* means, and that is why the Lord uses it — because it is an apt illustration of burial.

Now, when someone receives Christ as his personal Savior and Lord, he has died to the old man and has received the nature of God. According to 2 Corinthians 5:17, he becomes a new creature in Christ Jesus. As an outward sign to the world that the person has died to the old man, we immerse him in a baptismal pool or a river. Putting him under the water represents the fact that the person — the old man — has died, and that we are now burying him. When we bring him up out of the water, this represents resurrection into newness of life.

The Sinful Nature Dead

Reread Romans 6:1-2, and notice another facet of our being crucified, dead, and buried with Christ.

> **What shall we say then? Shall we continue in sin, that grace may abound?**
> **God forbid. How shall we, that are dead to sin....**

In the Greek, the word *sin* in these verses is literally "sinful nature." It does not mean sin in terms of an act of sin, like telling a lie or stealing something. It means sin as a way of life. We can, therefore, read Romans 6:1-4 like this:

What shall we say then? Shall we continue in the sinful nature, that grace may abound?

God forbid. How shall we, that are dead to the sinful nature, live any longer therein?

Know ye not, that so many of us as were baptized into Jesus Christ were baptized into His death?

Therefore we are buried with him....

Here it is again: **Therefore we are buried with him.... How are we buried with Him? ... by baptism into death: that like as Christ was raised from the dead by the glory of the Father, even so we also should walk in newness of life.**

That means if we have been identified with Christ in His death and burial, we should also be identified with Him in His resurrection. And the way we are supposed to be identified with Christ in His resurrection is that the life we live when we come up from the water should be diametrically opposed to the life we were living before we accepted Christ.

We were living in sin, doing the works of Satan and the works of the flesh. We should now be doing the works of the spirit, and walking in line with the Word of God. There should be a difference in the way you walk, talk, think, and act. If there is no difference, you need to examine yourself, and find out whether you are really walking in the spirit or are still walking in the flesh.

Romans 6:5:

For if we have been planted together in the likeness of his death....

Notice the word *likeness*. It indicates that Paul is now talking about a symbol. **Likeness of his death** refers to water baptism, a symbol of being dead, buried, then coming out of death into newness of life.

Romans 6:5-6:

For if we have been planted together in the likeness of his death, we shall be also in the likeness of his resurrection:

Knowing this, that our old man is crucified with him, that the body of sin [again, this should be the sinful nature] **might be destroyed, that henceforth we should not serve sin** [here the word sin is correct].

In Romans 6:6, the word *destroyed* in the Greek does not have the same meaning that it has in English. *Destroyed* in English means the thing that is destroyed is annihilated, and we think of it as though it no longer exists.

That cannot be true here, however. If the sinful nature were completely gone, there would never be any danger of our sinning anymore. There would be no Christians shacking up. There would be no fornication or adultery in the Body of Christ, as well as no stealing, lying, or any other act of sin. That would be nice, but we have not arrived there yet by a longshot.

Destroyed in Romans 6:6, in the Greek, means "to render inactive." It does not mean that you cannot sin. It simply means that you do not have to sin. However, the *possibility* of yielding to sin is still there.

Romans 6:7:

For he that is dead is freed from sin.

Let me stick a pin here, because there are certain brothers and sisters who read this passage of Scripture and say, "Oh, honey, I'm saved, sanctified, filled with the Holy Ghost, and free from sin." They are implying that there is no way in the world they can sin. Again, that is not the case.

Freed from sin means you do not have to sin anymore, but you can sin if you want to. If you are honest about it, you will be able to say you have sinned as a Christian, and that you knew it was sin when you did it, but you did it because you could get away with it.

I have done that myself, and I do not say that with any relish. I thought it was a part of being human to yield to sin. I was sorry and repented afterwards, but I went back and did it again. I thought I would have to continue like that for the rest of my life, because the churches I went to did not tell me that I was free in the sense that sin had no more legal dominion over me.

However, when I learned sin had no legal hold over me any longer, and I learned how to use the name of Jesus and to resist the devil, I took the finger of the Word of God and said, "Satan, in the name of Jesus, I bind you, and I refuse to bow my knee to you any longer." And I was free.

Sin is still around because the devil is still around. You will never be in a situation where there is no more temptation to sin until either the devil is taken out of the way, or you are in heaven with God. As long as you are in this physical realm, it is possible for you to sin. The good news, however, is that you have the ability and the authority not to yield to it.

Romans 6:8-11:

Now if we be dead with Christ, we believe that we shall also live with him:

Knowing that Christ being raised from the dead dieth no more; death hath no more dominion over him.

For in that he died, he died unto sin [that is, the sinful nature] once: but in that he liveth, he liveth unto God.

Likewise, reckon ye also yourselves to be dead indeed unto sin [the sinful nature]....

Do you know what reckon means? It means to count yourself the same as Christ. Reckon means to count yourself as being dead. You are really not dead in the natural, but you should look at yourself as though you were dead. If you do that, you will not yield to the sinful nature.

Let me give you an illustration to show you what I mean. Imagine a man coming home from working in an oil field. He is dirty, grimy, dingy. He goes home, gets in his shower, uses his favorite deodorant soap to clean himself up. He then puts on a brand-new pair of clean shorts, a clean white T-shirt, a white dress shirt and tie, a white suit, white socks, and white shoes. After he is dressed, the man goes out to meet his girl. He is Mr. Clean now. He is so clean that he almost looks metallic when the sun strikes him.

The man walks down the highway and comes to a bend in the road. Around the bend, he notices some people working in a hole by the side of the road, and something shooting up and falling from the hole. As he gets closer, the man can see that the men in the hole are trying to cap a broken oil line.

As the man draws near, one of the workers looks up and sees him coming. The worker says, "Hey, you. Come over here and help us. We're having a little problem getting a cap on this line. I have to hold one side, and my partner here is holding the other side, but we need someone else to give us a hand, and one of our crew just left because he got ill. Would you please get in this hole with us and help us?"

The man says, "What? Me get down there in that grime and oil and mess? Can't you see I'm clean? Can't you see my white suit, my white shirt and tie, and my white shoes? I'm not going to get down there in that mess. You had better forget about it." He then trudges down the road.

Why does he do and say that? Because he knows he is clean, and for him to get in that hole will mess him up. Since he has control, he says, "No," and walks on by.

Here is the same situation, but with a different man. This man has just come from working in the oil fields. He is grimy, dirty, and smelly. As he gets to the place where the workers are trying to cap that oil line, they see him and call him over. They ask him to help them out, and this man says, "Why, sure." He is just as filthy as they are, and he cannot get any dirtier than he already is, so he figures he might as well help them out.

Can you see the difference?

If you are already living in sin, and you are a sinner, it is no problem for you to continue getting dirty because you cannot get much dirtier than you already are. However, when you are clean, it is very easy to say, "Hey, can't you see I'm clean? I'm going to stay clean, so you will have to find someone else to help you."

Spiritually, you ought to act like that clean person did. When the blood of Jesus cleans you up, and the Holy Spirit washes out all the sin stains of your life, you need to walk down the road of life and say, "No, Satan, I can't sin. I'm clean by the blood of the Lamb!"

We Are Declared Righteous

In Romans 6:6, we read that "the body of sin," or of our sinful nature, was destroyed or rendered inactive. We could also read "the body of sin" as the body of spiritual death. When the body of sin was rendered inactive by Christ's paying our penalty for us, mankind was released from spiritual death.

Also, after Jesus paid our penalty, we stood before God justified, or declared righteous, on the basis of what Jesus did through His redemptive work. We were made, and now are, the righteousness of God in Christ.

What exactly does that mean? Socrates, who is called the father of philosophy, once said that no man could speak intelligently on any subject unless he first of all defined the terms he used. Let me therefore define what I mean by *righteousness*.

Righteousness means the ability of you as a person to stand in the presence of God as free from sin and condemnation, as though there had never been any spiritual death in you from the time of your conception. It is as though you had never done anything wrong and were absolutely perfect.

The reason we can approach God as righteousness is that we have been cleansed by the blood of Jesus. We have the ability, because of what Jesus did and our identification with Him, to stand in the presence of God as God's free men, without any sense of condemnation or spiritual inferiority.

The fact we can stand like that in God's presence is what I consider to be one of the most important truths a Christian can have in his personal life. It has set me free in many areas. However, we must learn to consistently keep this truth in mind if we are to live victorious lives in Christ Jesus. That process can be summed up as learning how to see ourselves as God sees us.

For a long time, I would look at myself and see only my flaws and mistakes. I thought that was the real me, so I would confess what I thought I saw. I did not realize it was the devil telling me all those things about myself, or that he did it to keep me in bondage.

If I had been looking in God's mirror, instead of in the mirror of life, I would have been looking into the face of Jesus. When I finally looked into God's mirror, I saw the glory of God in the face of Jesus, and I saw myself as God actually sees me.

Remember, God does not see you like you see yourself in the bathroom mirror. God sees you through Jesus. When God sees you through Jesus, you look very good, because Jesus looks very good.

When you see yourself as God sees you, it will raise you out of the quagmire of an inferiority complex. It will raise you above the level of all the devil says you cannot accomplish and all the other garbage he has been telling you all your life. It will make you an "I can" person instead of an "I can't" person — "I can" in the sense of **I can do all things through Christ which strengtheneth me** (Phil. 4:13).

Approaching the Throne

Before I came into the knowledge of being the righteousness of God in Christ and how to walk by faith, when I approached the throne of God through prayer, I did so with fear and trepidation. I did so feeling unworthy, wondering if God was going to strike me dead for daring to lift my eyes to His throne. Perhaps you know of others who have done this also. Do you know why we did it? Because we did not understand righteousness.

I did not know that because of what Jesus did, it cleared the record on my behalf, or that it gave me the right to stand in the presence of God as His son. You do not have to apologize when you go in to see your mother and father. You have a right to go in and see them because they are your parents. You can do the same thing with God. Because of what Jesus did for us, He is *your* heavenly Father, too.

I do not apologize anymore. I break right in on the throne room and say, "Father, listen. I have this little thing that arose down here on earth, and I need thus-and-so."

The heavenly Father says, "Alright, son. What does My Word say?"

I tell Him, "Father, Your Word says that what things soever I desire, when I pray, believe that I receive it, and I'll have it."

The Father tells me, "Hop to it, son." And when I put God's Word into action, I get what I ask for."

Hebrews 4:14-16:

Seeing then that we have a great high priest, that is passed into the heavens, Jesus the Son of God, let us hold fast our profession.

For we have not an high priest which cannot be touched with the feeling of our infirmities; but was in all points tempted like as we are, yet without sin.

Let us therefore come boldly unto the throne of grace, that we may obtain mercy, and find grace to help in time of need.

He does not say to come crawling in on your hands and knees apologizing. He says, **Let us therefore come boldly** — not arrogantly, not irreverently, but boldly, as though you have a right to be there. And you do have a right to be there, because of Jesus.

4

Made Alive With Christ

The fourth step in our identification with Christ is, **I was made alive with Christ**. When Jesus was made alive, we were made alive. Jesus was crucified, He died, and He was buried, but He was also resurrected and made alive. He did not stay dead, and that is the uniqueness of Christianity. Every "prophet" of every other persuasion who said he spoke for God is dead, but Jesus is a living Savior. The tomb is empty.

Colossians 2:13:
> **And you, being dead in your sins and the uncircumcision of your flesh, hath he quickened together with him** [that is, with Jesus], **having forgiven you all trespasses.**

The word *quicken* in the original Greek means to make alive, that whatever is quickened is made a living thing. We could read Colossians 2:13 like this:

> **And you, being dead in your sins and the uncircumcision of your flesh, hath he made alive together with him, having forgiven you all trespasses.**

Physical resurrection could not possibly be what is referred to in this verse, because we have never experienced physical resurrection. The only way we will experience that will be if we die before Jesus comes back.

Also, some Christians will be alive when Jesus returns, so they will never experience physical resurrection. Yes, their bodies will be translated and changed from corruptible to incorruptible in the twinkling of an eye. There is no question about that. However, they will not have to be physically resurrected. The only way you have to be physically resurrected is if you have physically died.

There is no way, therefore, that we could be identified with Jesus in physical resurrection. When Colossians 2:13 mentions being "quickened together with him," it is referring to spiritual resurrection.

Earlier in this book, I mentioned that Jesus had to die spiritually, to be identified with us in our spiritual death, so that He could die physically to pay the penalty due for those who were spiritually dead. After divine justice was satisfied, Jesus was quickened or made alive in His spirit, and He became the first man to experience the new birth.

When Jesus was born out of spiritual death into spiritual life, we were born out of that death at the same time in the mind of God. God saw us born again as Jesus was born again out of spiritual death. That has not physically happened for everyone, because not everyone has accepted Jesus as his personal Savior and Lord. In the mind of God it has happened, however. So every individual has the right to receive Christ as his personal Savior and to experience the new birth.

Ephesians 2:5:

Even when we were dead in sins, hath quickened us together with Christ, (by grace ye are saved.)

Notice again that we are identified with Christ, quickened or made alive with Him.

And Winning Dominion Over Physical Death

When God raised Christ from the dead, He caused Him to have dominion not only over spiritual death, but over physical death, as well.

Acts 13:33-34:

God hath fulfilled the same unto us their children, in that he hath raised up Jesus again; as it is also written in the second psalm, Thou art my Son, this day have I begotten thee.

And as concerning that he [God] raised him [Christ] up from the dead, now no more to return to corruption, he said on this wise, I will give you the sure mercies of David.

Corruption alerts us to the fact that God is now including physical death. Jesus will never suffer corruption so, according to Acts 13:33-34, Jesus has authority in the physical realm as far as physical death is concerned.

It was never the will, plan, and purpose of God for His creatures to die physically. Remember, spiritual death and physical death always go hand in hand, because physical death is the end result of spiritual death. Spiritual death came first, and it opened the door for physical death to come forth.

Now that Jesus has overturned spiritual death, there is coming a day when physical death will also be overturned. In the meantime, we who have been identified with Christ in being made new spiritually, also now have authority over physical death, in that physical death cannot lord it over us or control us.

Do not misunderstand me here. You will die physically unless you are alive when Jesus returns. However, you should die only when you are ready to, within the framework of God's Word.

After Noah came out of the Ark after the Flood, God said the number of a man's days shall be 120 years. You should be able to live 120 years — and I do not mean 120 years, and crippled, blind, deaf, cataracted, or arthritic. You do not have to be any of those things, because the Bible says Moses was 120 when he died physically, and that his eyes were as strong as an eagle's, and his back was as straight as a ramrod. Also, when the children of Israel went into the Promised Land, old Caleb told Joshua, "I want that mountain." Joshua said, "That's a mighty big mountain, Caleb. Are you able to take it?" Caleb told him, "I'm 85 years old, but I'm just as good as when I was 40."

The fact that you are old chronologically does not mean you have to be decrepit, bent out of shape, or wasted away. We have accepted that as the norm; therefore, Satan has accommodated us according to our way of thinking. But if you go by what the Word of God says, the Lord will keep you from having those infirmities come upon you.

Romans 6:9-10:

Knowing that Christ being raised from the dead dieth no more; death hath no more dominion over him.

For in that he died, he died unto sin once: but in that he liveth, he liveth unto God.

As I said, spiritual death and physical death have no more dominion over Jesus. It has no more control over Him, and we are identified with Christ in that. Spiritual death and physical death have no more dominion over us. In other words, death cannot rush in like a flood and take us out if we do not allow it to.

This is a tremendously important concept, one that is revolutionary from the standpoint of the traditional church. In fact, some preachers call the idea heretical and false doctrine. But it is Bible, however, and it can easily be supported by the scriptures.

Death — the Enemy

1 Corinthians 15:24-26:

Then cometh the end, when he [Christ] shall have delivered up the kingdom to God, even the Father; when he shall have put down all rule and all authority and power.

For he must reign, till he hath put all enemies under his feet.

The last enemy that shall be destroyed is death.

Physical and spiritual death are enemies. Death is not a friend. We have accused God of killing people for many years, but if God were the one doing that, He would be our enemy and not our friend. Jesus Himself says in John 10:10, **The thief cometh not, but for to steal, and to kill, and to destroy: I am come that they might have life, and that they might have it more abundantly.**

If the only reason the thief comes is to steal, kill, and destroy, and if Jesus came to bring us life, not death, then death does not come from God. If death does not come from God, we do not have to accept it on death's terms.

Because of Adam's sin, physical death is in the world today. And because of that, everyone will physically die, except those who are alive when Jesus returns. However, for the Christian who is informed in the Word of God, death should simply be the vehicle by which we make the transfer out of the physical realm into the spiritual realm to be with Jesus. That should be after we have lived a long, satisfying life and are ready to be with the Lord. There should be no fear involved, any dread, or any of the other things we typically associate with physical death.

Hebrews 2:9:
> **But we see Jesus, who was made a little lower than the angels for the suffering of death, crowned with glory and honour; that he by the grace of God should taste death for every man.**

Death in this verse refers to spiritual death. Jesus tasted spiritual death so that every man could be released from it. Again, that does not mean every man will be saved, but it means every man has the opportunity to be saved. As John 1:12 puts it, **But as many as** received him, to them gave he power [authority, right, or privilege] to become the sons of God, even to them that believe on his name.

Now notice what is said in Hebrews 2:10-15:

> For it became him, for whom are all things, and by whom are all things, in bringing many sons unto glory, to make the captain of their salvation perfect through sufferings.
>
> For both he that sanctifieth and they who are sanctified are all of one: for which cause he is not ashamed to call them brethren,
>
> Saying, I will declare thy name unto my brethren, in the midst of the church will I sing praise unto thee.
>
> And again, I will put my trust in him. And again, Behold I and the children which God hath given me.
>
> Forasmuch then as the children are partakers of flesh and blood, he also likewise took part of the same; that through death he might destroy him that had the power of death, that is, the devil;
>
> And deliver them who through fear of death were all their lifetime subject to bondage.

You ought to shout about that. **That though death he might destroy him that had the power of death, that is, the devil.** Not God, not the angels, but the devil had that power. And as far as Christians are concerned, Satan does not have that power over us any more. He still has it for the sinner, but he has no legal right to lord it over the Body of Christ.

However, if you do not know this and if you do not know your rights in Christ, the devil will come in like a flood and try to put death on you, because he is a usurper. And if you are ignorant enough to accept his deception, he will kill you, and there will be nothing God will be able to do about it.

"Well now, Brother Price, what about Brother So-and-so, and Sister So-and-so, and Bishop So-and-so? They were all lovely saints of God, and they died."

You are right. They were lovely saints of God. But they were probably just like you and I were at one time, not knowing their rights in Christ. Their churches probably did not teach them their rights. Because of ignorance, Satan took advantage of them. God says in Hosea 4:6, **My people are destroyed for lack of knowledge** — lack of knowledge of the Word of God. This is an area where ignorance can literally kill you.

First Among Many Brethren

Romans 8:29:
For whom he did foreknow, he also did predestinate to be conformed to the image of his Son, that he might be the firstborn among many brethren.

Notice the word *firstborn*. When you hear the word *first* in anything, it implies there is more than one.

This verse could not be talking about Jesus' being physically the firstborn, because there were people living on the earth before He came. It also could not be talking about being raised from the dead, because Jesus was not the first person who was raised from the dead. In fact, we have a record of Jesus Himself raising at least three people from the dead during His earthly ministry.

Colossians 1:18:

And he is the head of the body, the church....

Who does **the body, the church** refer to? Us. Any born-again Believer is a part of the Body of Christ — the Church — and Christ is the head over the Church. Keep reading, and you will see why Jesus is called the firstborn.

And he is the head of the body, the church: who is the beginning, the firstborn from the dead; that in all things he might have the preeminence.

The word *beginning* implies the start of something. Then we read, **... the firstborn from the dead.** That would not mean being the firstborn from physical death, because there were people raised from the dead before Jesus was raised. What it means is that Jesus was the first person raised from spiritual death, and because He was the first, He is the head of the Body. He is the first born-again man, but thank God He is not the last one.

When God looks at us, He sees us as one Body with many members. We are conformed to the image of Christ, and He loves each of us the same way He loves Jesus. As Jesus phrases it in John 17:23, **I in them, and thou in me, that they may be made perfect in one; and that the world may know that thou hast sent me, and hast loved them, as thou hast loved me.**

Predestined to Live or Die Spiritually?

Romans 8:30:

Moreover whom he did predestinate, them he also called: and whom he called, them he also justified: and whom he justified, them he also glorified.

Let me explain something, because sometimes people misunderstand the term predestination. No one is predestined in the sense that God has programmed you to either be saved or lost, and you have no choice about it. God does already know who will accept Jesus as Savior and Lord, because He is God and He knows everything, but His knowing does not affect the choice of accepting Christ or not.

The only thing God has predestined relative to our salvation is that when God gets through with us, all us Christians will look just like Jesus. That is all predestination means here.

Ephesians 1:5,11:

Having predestinated us unto the adoption of children by Jesus Christ to himself, according to the good pleasure of his will...

In whom also we have obtained an inheritance, being predestinated according to the purpose of him who worketh all things after the counsel of his own will.

Again, having predestinated us does not mean God has programmed us to receive or to not receive Christ as our personal Savior. What it means is that, if

I adopt Christ, God will accept me as His child, I will be conformed to the image of His Son, and I will have an inheritance.

Your salvation is based on you. God has provided it. He has made it available to you. Whosoever will, let him come. It is just that simple.

Suffering With Christ?

Romans 8:17:

> **And if children, then heirs; heirs of God, and joint-heirs with Christ; if so be that we suffer with him, that we may be also glorified together.**

Many people think that, when they become Christians, they have to stay poor, sick, whipped, and defeated in order to suffer for the Lord. That is not what the Bible says about suffering, and it should not be our attitude about it either.

Before you get uptight about the word *suffer*, ask yourself this question: How did Jesus suffer? If you read the four Gospels, you will find that Jesus never went without a meal. He never went without a place to stay, or a means of transportation. He was always able to pay His taxes, and He never went around sick. He never suffered any of those things.

There was only one way Jesus suffered. He was ridiculed by the religious leaders and misunderstood by those who were closest to Him. Jesus never had any problems with the people He ministered to. All of His problems came from His family and from the religious leaders of that day.

That is where we, as followers of Christ, will have to suffer, as well. There will be people who will call you fanatical, crazy, and everything else but a child of God. That may include your friends, your family, your relatives, and the religious establishment. Do you know what the Bible says about Jesus? It says, "And the common people heard him gladly" (Mark 12:37). I am glad I am one of the common folk, and you should be, also.

Look again at Romans 8:17, and notice a couple of other things.

> **And if children, then heirs; heirs of God, and joint-heirs with Christ; if so be that we suffer with him, that we may be also glorified together.**

First, notice that **we suffer with him.** We do not suffer for the Lord; we suffer *with* Him. In other words, when we put up with all the lying, persecution, and misrepresentation from other people, we do not have to think we are taking it alone. Jesus tells us in Matthew 28:20, **... and, lo, I am with you alway** [or always], **even unto the end of the world.** He knows what we are going through. He is standing there with us, through the person of the Holy Spirit, and He is ready to comfort us and help us through those times of persecution. That is why one of the names for the Holy Spirit is **the Comforter.**

Joint-Heirs of Life

Something else to notice in Romans 8:17 is that we are **heirs of God, and joint-heirs with Christ.** We were legally born out of death into life with Him. For that reason, God tells us to count ourselves as though we were dead to our sinful nature, because we are alive unto God. No matter what the devil or anyone else tries to bring up about our past, we are free from it, because we are alive to God. All we have to do is stand on the Word, and we can remain free.

1 Corinthians 15:22:

> **For as in Adam all die, even so in Christ shall all be made alive.**

That *all* is actually qualified. It means whosoever will accept Jesus as his or her Savior and Lord. As I said earlier, not everyone will accept Jesus, but everyone has the opportunity to do so. For those who do accept Him, they will be made alive in Him. They can be the recipients of all the blessings that accrue as a result of what Jesus did, as well as be free from Satan's dominion.

Changing Spiritual Parents

Whether you realize it or not, everyone has a spiritual parentage. If you have not accepted Christ as your personal Savior, Satan is your spiritual father. There are only two spiritual families in the earth-realm — the family of God and the family of Satan. You are automatically in one or the other.

When you have accepted Christ as your personal Savior, Satan is no longer your spiritual father. Your spiritual father becomes Almighty God. As a result of that, Satan no longer has any legal jurisdiction or control over you.

Colossians 1:12-13:

Giving thanks unto the Father, which hath made us meet [or able] to be partakers of the inheritance of the saints in light:

Who hath delivered us from the power of darkness, and hath translated us into the kingdom of his dear Son.

Remember, however, that Satan is a usurper. He is a thief, a murderer, and a robber. If you give him an inch, he will take 25 miles. What you need to do is learn your kingdom rights and privileges, and begin to operate in them. That will put Satan on the outside, and he will have no dominion over you whatsoever.

Under Our Feet

After Christ had been made spiritually alive and released from Satan's authority, the next step was to put off from Himself, and us, the forces of Satan.

Ephesians 1:20-23:

Which he [God] **wrought in Christ, when he
raised him from the dead, and set him at his own
right hand in the heavenly places,**
**Far above all principality, and power, and might,
and dominion, and every name that is named, not
only in this world, but also in that which is to come:**
**And hath put all things under his feet, and gave
him to be the head over all things to the church,**
**Which is his body, the fulness of him that filleth
all in all.**

Notice what Christ's body is: **... the church, which
is his body.** We are the body. Every one of us who has
accepted Jesus as Savior and Lord is seen by God as the
Body of Christ.

The Bible says that Jesus has been made the head
over all things to the Church, which is His Body. It also
says that as a result of Christ being raised from the
dead and defeating Satan and all of the demon hosts,
God the Father has put all things under the feet of
Christ. All things include poverty, sickness, fear, hate,
want, and destruction. You name it — it is under
Christ's feet.

God does not make headless bodies, or bodiless
heads. Whenever He sees the body, He sees the head. If
Christ is the head and we are the body, that means all
things are under our feet. It means we are on top, no
matter what the devil may throw at us.

This is a legal, contractual, covenant privilege we
have. However, you as an individual Christian will
never walk in the fullness of it until you believe it in
your heart, confess it with your mouth, and act on it in
your life. Even though, legally, it is yours, you have to

talk it, think it, sleep it, eat it, drink it, walk it. It has to be an everyday part of your life. That makes the difference between winning and losing.

5

Raised With Christ

When the demands of divine justice were satisfied, and God said, "It is enough. Man is now free," Jesus was made spiritually alive in the bowels of hell itself. Once that happened, Jesus came up from hell to the garden tomb, and picked up His body. That lets us know about our next step in our identification with Christ: **I was raised with Christ.**

Ephesians 2:4-6:
> **But God, who is rich in mercy, for his great love wherewith he loved us,**
>
> **Even when we were dead in sins, hath quick-ened us** [or made us alive] **together with Christ, (by grace ye are saved;)**
>
> **And hath raised us up together, and made us sit together in heavenly places in Christ Jesus.**

Raised up together with Christ is where God sees us, and it is where we need to learn to see ourselves. This does not mean you become so heavenly minded that you become no earthly good. There is a place or balance where you can be heavenly minded enough to function in the heavenly realm, and also be earthly minded enough to be able to function in that realm, as well.

When you see yourself raised up and seated in heavenly places with Christ Jesus, there will be many things the devil has been dishing out to you that you will not take any longer. You will begin saying, "I'm going to put this off, in Jesus' name. You can't do this to me, Satan. You have no authority here. I'm seated together in heavenly places with Christ Jesus."

When you think of yourself as seated in heavenly places with Christ Jesus, people cannot hurt your feelings any more. You get to a point where it does not matter what people say, because you are living above the circumstances of life. You still may not like it when people talk badly about you, but you will think, "It does not matter. They do not know me, anyway."

Sometimes you can get extremely angry and frustrated because people misunderstand you and talk unkindly about you. However, do not yield to the temptation to strike back. That is exactly what Satan wants you to do. Instead, do what Jesus said to do. Pray for them. And when you do that, it will be like heaping coals of fire on top of their heads.

Remember also, the Bible says that no weapon the enemy forms against you shall prosper, and that God will condemn every tongue that rises against you in judgment. But you cannot do that unless you are living in the heavenly realm. If you live strictly in the earth-realm, you will be tempted to fight back the same way you believe people are fighting you.

Instead of fighting back, keep living the Word and talking the Word. Be an example of a Believer, and let them talk and criticize. God is well able to take care of the critics. If they misunderstand you, do not feel bad.

You will be in good company. In fact, you will be in the best company of all, because they misunderstood Jesus. We are in Christ because we are identified with Him, and that is the reason the devil is on our case.

Spirits, Not People, Are Your Enemy

You need to realize that our enemy is a spiritual enemy. Read this carefully, and do not forget it: Men are not your problem. Satan will use men to infuriate and aggravate you, but do not look at them as your problem. Look at the spirit creature who is manipulating people as your problem.

That is why Jesus said from the cross, **Father, forgive them, for they know not what they do.** They really do not know, because they have been deceived by the wicked one.

Ephesians 6:12:

For we wrestle not against flesh and blood, but against principalities, against powers, against the rulers of the darkness of this world, against spiritual wickedness in high places.

Can you see how the devil has deceived people? White people are not your problem. Neither Black people, Native Americans, nor Asians are your problems. Neither Baptists, Methodists, nor anyone else are your problems.

Flesh and blood is not your problem. Evil spirits, Satan, and demon forces are what you should be on the look-out for. Those are the rulers Jesus Christ disarmed and displayed as His conquest in the throne room of hell. They have no power or legal authority in the Christians's life unless we allow them to have power or authority over what belongs to us.

Colossians 2:15:

> And having spoiled principalities and powers, he made a shew of them openly, triumphing over them in it.

Having spoiled principalities and powers in the Greek literally means that the principalities and powers were stripped of all badges or signs of rank or power. It would be like what filmmakers sometimes show in movies in which an officer is found guilty of a crime against his nation. You watch the officer's superior publicly take away his gold braids, badges, medals, and other military insignias and badges of rank. When everything is over, the officer is not even a buck private anymore. He has been stripped of rank.

When Jesus spoiled principalities and powers, all the demons in hell and all the angels in heaven were present. That is what it means when Colossians 2:15 says Jesus "made a shew of them openly." They watched Him strip Satan and his demon forces of all the power they had. In fact, when He was finished, Satan was left stark naked.

Those demon forces have been defeated, and now we, the Body of Christ, are the victors. We will not get any benefit from Christ's victory, however, until we take our authority, rise on the wings of faith, take the Word of God, which is the sword of the Spirit, and go forth to conquer in the name of Jesus.

Jesus Triumphed Because of Us

Here is a spiritual truth that will bless your heart, because it is absolutely beautiful. If you do not get it right away, just meditate on it for a while and let it sink into your spirit. The spiritual truth is this: It was only because of our identification with Christ that Jesus triumphed over Satan.

Why do I say that? Because Jesus was always greater than Satan. Do you think Jesus came into this earth-realm to defeat Satan just to prove He was greater? Friend, He was greater from time immemorial.

Jesus did it for us. He came down here and took upon Himself human flesh for us. He walked this earth and took the jeers, sarcasm, and false accusations of men for only one purpose — *to defeat Satan so we could get the benefit out of it.*

Satan does not want us to know he is defeated. He does not want the Church to know it, and he has infiltrated what we call "religion" and made it appear as though he is bigger than God. Nevertheless, Satan is a defeated foe.

The only reason the world is continuing in the way it is, is that God loves you. The only reason God has not pushed the red button on the whole human situation is that He wants you in His family. He wants you saved, and He is allowing things to go on so you will have time to get your game together. It is because God so loved the world. Otherwise, He would have "red-buttoned" it a long time ago.

6
Seated With Christ

The final step in our identification with Christ is, **I was seated with Christ**. Notice our progression in these six steps: crucified, dead, buried, made alive, raised, seated. This is a complete cycle from defeat to victory.

Once you, as a Believer, get a true picture of this cycle — the fact that you are identified with Christ in every aspect of this cycle and the fact you are seated with Christ — it will be impossible for you to be defeated in any area of life. You are a winner. That is how God sees you, and this is what the Scriptures say you are.

This is what should make you bold in Christ — the fact you are a winner with Him. That is not having a superior attitude. It is having a Word-oriented attitude. I do not feel superior in the sense of looking down on people and saying, "I am superior, and you are inferior." It is simply a matter of knowing who I am, because my Heavenly Father told me who I am in His Word.

If I asked you what your name was, you would not hesitate for a minute to tell me. You would not hem, haw, stumble, and say, "Well, I am not sure what my mother named me. They have been telling me all these years what I have been going by. Maybe that is my name, but I am not really sure."

Does knowing your name mean you have a superior attitude? Of course not. Well, when they ask me what my name is, I tell them it is *Winner*. That is what God names me in His Word. Not Loser, but Winner. He told me I am a winner, so I act like it — and it feels good to win!

We started to discuss this in the last chapter, when we read and discussed Ephesians 2:4-6. We will look at those verses of Scripture again, in somewhat more detail than we did last time.

The View From the Right Hand of God

But God, who is rich in mercy, for his great love wherewith he loved us,

Even when we were dead in sins, hath quickened us together with Christ, (by grace ye are saved;)

And hath raised us up together, and made us sit together in heavenly places in Christ Jesus.

If we are identified with Christ in His being seated at the right hand of the Father, that is where God sees us. When He looks to His right, He not only sees Jesus seated there, but He sees you and me seated there, as well.

As I said in the last chapter, when you begin to see yourself seated with Jesus, all the problems you thought were so big will not seem so large. Also, keep this in mind. What does the word *together* mean? It means you and at least one other person. If you have been raised together with Jesus to sit in heavenly places, it means you are raised up with Him.

Notice also the word *made* in verse six. *Made* clears up any doubts, speculation, or debate on whether or not we are seated with Christ in heavenly places. He *made* us sit. We are together with Christ, so that means Jesus in not seated alone on the right hand of God.

The word *us* is used twice in verse six. Whenever you see that word, you should substitute your name for it. Learn how to personalize the scriptures, put them in your setting, and see yourself as a part of what is being said. In fact, go back and reread the verses over and over; and put your name where appropriate. Let them get down into your spirit, as you get a spiritual image of yourself sitting in heaven at the right hand of the Father God.

When you get that picture in your spirit and keep it there, you will begin to see yourself as a champion, and you will stop accepting second best. You will cease from accepting defeat. You will think, "I am together with Christ. I can't lose. I can only win, because I am with the champion, Jesus Christ."

Too many people have a spiritual inferiority complex, because they have been looking at the picture Satan has been presenting of them. All the time they have been looking at that picture, God has been trying to get in and tell them, "What you look like is Jesus." When you see God's picture of you, you cannot lose.

We Have Christ's Authority

Before Jesus went back to heaven, He informed His disciples of the authority that had been vested in

Him as a result of His being crucified, dead, buried, made alive, and risen. After He told them, He immediately delegated that authority to His Body, the Church.

Matthew 28:18:
> And Jesus came and spake unto them, saying, All power is given unto me in heaven and in earth.

The word *power* in verse 18 is the Greek word *exousia*, which means "authority, right, or privilege." It literally means you have the right to do something. Notice that all power was given to Jesus **in heaven and in earth.** Right after He said this, Jesus physically went to heaven, so what good did it do for God to give Jesus all power in heaven and in earth?

It actually did a lot of good, because God gave that authority for His family, the Body of Christ. That means He gave it for us!

That authority is for us. Jesus went back to heaven, but He left His Body on the earth to finish His work. Notice what Matthew 28:19-20 says that work constitutes.

> Go ye therefore, and teach all nations, baptizing them in the name of the Father, and of the Son, and of the Holy Ghost:
> Teaching them to observe all things whatsoever I have commanded you: and, lo, I am with you alway, even unto the end of the world. Amen.

Every time you read the word *therefore*, you need to stop and consider what it is there for. The word *therefore* means "for this reason." If you do not consider the reason alluded to by *therefore*, how will you know why you are supposed to do what comes after it?

Reread Matthew 28:18-20, and look more closely at what *therefore* in verse 19 refers to.

> **And Jesus came and spake to them, saying, All power** [authority, right, or privilege] **is given unto me in heaven and in earth.**
>
> **Go ye therefore** [meaning based on the fact that all authority in heaven and in earth is in my hand, you go]**, and teach all nations, baptizing them in the name of the Father, and of the Son, and of the Holy Ghost:**
>
> **Teaching them to observe all things whatsoever I have commanded you: and, lo, I am with you alway, even unto the end of the world. Amen.**

I do not know why the Church has failed to do this. The Church has not taught the people the Word of God. It has been preaching, but it has not done much teaching. This is why many Christians are ignorant of who they are in Christ. This is why Satan can keep them under control, in the mud, the muck, and the mire — because the Church has not taught them who God says they are in Christ.

Under Your Feet

In Acts 2:34-35, we can see some very important things about the authority that was given to us. This is on the day of Pentecost, and Peter is speaking.

> **For David is not ascended unto the heavens: but he saith himself, The Lord said unto my Lord, Sit thou on my right hand,**
> **Until I make thy foes thy footstool.**

A footstool is something you put your feet on, and anything you put your feet on is usually designed to go underneath your feet.

Hebrews 1:13:

> **But to which of the angels said he at any time, Sit on my right hand, until I make thine enemies thy footstool?**

Hebrews 10:12-13:

> **But this man [Jesus], after he had offered one sacrifice for sins for ever, sat down on the right hand of God;**
> **From henceforth expecting till his enemies be made his footstool.**

These verses say basically the same thing Peter does in Acts 2:34-35. Why is Christ sitting, waiting for His enemies to be made His footstool?

Whether you realize it or not — and I am sure many have not thought of it — for the last 1,900 years or so, Jesus Christ has been exercising His faith. He has been believing He is going to do exactly what He left us equipped to do — and He equipped us to make His enemies His footstool.

At the moment, Jesus cannot do anything to that effect, because the Father has told Him to sit on His right hand until His enemies are made His footstool.

You may ask, "How is that going to get done, then? Jesus is seated at the right hand of the Father, and the Father is seated on the central throne."

The only part of the Godhead in the earth-realm today is the Holy Spirit. However, the Holy Spirit does not do anything by Himself. He works only through vessels He is permitted to fill and empower.

That means those vessels which are filled with the power of the Holy Spirit will have to bring the foes of Jesus down, and make them His footstool before He comes back.

Ephesians 1:19-21:

And what is the exceeding greatness of his power to usward who believe, according to the working of his mighty power,

Which he wrought in Christ, when he raised him from the dead, and set him at his own right hand in the heavenly places,

Far above all principality, and power, and might, and dominion, and every name that is named, not only in this world, but also in that which is to come.

All things include sickness, disease, poverty, fear, unworthiness, hate, prejudice, strife, inability, lack, want, and any other negative thing you can think of. Notice what the next two verses tell us.

Ephesians 1:22-23:

And hath put all things under his feet, and gave him to be the head over all things to the church,

Which is his body, the fulness of him that filleth all in all.

Notice that the Father put all things under Christ's feet, then made Him to be the head of the Body, the Church. Your feet are not attached to your head. They are attached to your body. That means God put all things under the feet of the Body of Christ, because the feet are located in the body. It means all things have been put under your feet, and if they are under your feet, you are on top.

We Are Winners, Not Losers

Are you winning in life? Are you winning over fear, or are you scared of airplanes, or tall buildings, or of the dark, or of cats, or of Black people moving in next to you? Are you scared? If you are scared, you are not a winner.

It does not mean you do not love the Lord, or that you will not go to heaven when you physically die. But it does mean you are whipped in this life, because you are not treating fear like it is under your feet. You are treating it like you are under its feet.

Are you sick? "Yes, Brother Price. I have been sick for 35 years. My ulcer is acting up again." In that case, you are not a winner. I did not say you did not love the Lord, or that you were not saved. All things are not under your feet, however, because an ulcer is a thing. It is a destructive, detrimental thing to your physical body, and your body is the temple of God. What makes you think that God wants to live inside of a house that does not have the plumbing or the electricity working right? Sickness and disease are under your feet.

Are your bills paid? I can tell you about a time when my bills were not paid, and I did not know how they were going to get paid. I lived from paycheck to paycheck, and all I did was carry my paycheck from my job to the finance company.

I do not do that anymore. In fact, since I started walking in line with God's Word, my needs have been abundantly supplied. God does not want you to be poor. Poverty is a thing, and it is under your feet.

Husbands and wives should be winning in their marital relationships. Some of them walk around the house without talking to one another. Others are separated and estranged from their spouses. It ought not to be so. Some parents cannot talk to their kids, and their kids do not want to talk to them.

I am well persuaded that Jesus Christ is not coming back until the Body of Christ takes its rightful place. You may think, "Jesus is going to come back and bail me out," and I do not mind being wrong, but I do not believe He will return until we use the authority God has given us to straighten our situations out. We read in several scriptures that Jesus is to sit at the right hand of the Father until His enemies are made His footstool. Until that happens, He is not coming back.

Satan is running amuck, and, unfortunately, he is governing most Christians, including preachers. He has a ring in their nose, a chain attached to the ring, and every time he pulls, they say, "I am sick. I can't do this. I can't do that. I don't know what I'm going to do."

Until you get all those negative things under your feet, you may as well unpack your bags and forget about being snatched out of here by the Rapture. There is much work to be done. There are many captives being held in the valley, bound by Satan with sin, spiritual death, disease, you name it.

We have the answer, praise God. We should be about our Father's business, rising on the wings of eagles, doing the work Christ gave us to do. He has given us the Spirit of God, the armor of God, the shield of faith, and the sword of the Spirit. How can we be defeated? The Bible says that if God is for us, who can be against us.

It Is Up to Us

We are identified with Christ. We were crucified, dead, buried, made alive, risen, and are seated in heavenly places with Christ Jesus. We should refuse to accept defeat, because Jesus refused to accept defeat, and He won the victory for us over anything the enemy can form against us.

Whether you win or lose is not up to God. Whether you are a success or a failure is not up to God. It is up to you. Your winning will be because of your operating in line with God's provisions through Jesus Christ, but the provisions have already been made.

Do you know what God is doing right now? God is on vacation. The Book of Hebrews says that God is resting from all His labors. Not only that, but He is having Jesus rest, also. That implies that the work they did for our benefit is already done on their part.

It is up to us. The ball is in our hand. The goal line is over there. If we make a touchdown, we make it; if we do not make it, we do not make it. Either way, the responsibility is now ours.

If you cannot say that Jesus Christ is your personal Savior and Lord, I would invite you to make Him the Lord of your life now. All you have to lose is this lousy, sinful life of worry, sickness, disease, poverty, fear, hate, and prejudice. You can leave all of that mess and live a life of joy, a life of peace, a life of victory, prosperity, and divine health.

If you want to accept this invitation, and settle your relationship with God, then pray the following prayer aloud:

Dear God, you said in Romans 10:9-10, "That if thou shalt confess with thy mouth the Lord Jesus, and shalt believe in thine heart that God hath raised him from the dead, thou shalt be saved. For with the heart man believeth unto righteousness; and with the mouth confession is made unto salvation."

I believe that Jesus Christ is Your Son, and that He was sent into the world as Savior to redeem my life. I believe that He died for me, and that He was raised from the dead for my justification. Jesus, be the Lord over my life. I confess you now as my Savior and Lord, and I do believe it with my heart. According to Your Word, I have now become the righteousness of God in Christ, and I am now saved. Thank you, Jesus.

If you made that confession, you are now a Christian. You are a new creature in Christ Jesus. You have been set free from sin and its dominion. God has forgotten your past sins. He does not remember them anymore.

Thank Him for His grace and walk on as a child of God. Determine in your heart to follow God's teachings as outlined in the Bible. As you learn to trust in His Word, you can expect to grow spiritually, and to learn what God's best is for your life.

For a complete list of books and tapes by
Dr. Frederick K.C. Price, or to receive his publication,
Ever Increasing Faith Messenger, write

Dr. Fred Price
Crenshaw Christian Center
P.O. Box 90000
Los Angeles CA 90009

BOOKS BY FREDERICK K.C. PRICE, PH.D.

HIGH FINANCE
(God's Financial Plan: Tithes and Offerings)

HOW FAITH WORKS
(In English and Spanish)

IS HEALING FOR ALL?

HOW TO OBTAIN STRONG FAITH
(Six Principles)

NOW FAITH IS

THE HOLY SPIRIT —
The Missing Ingredient

FAITH, FOOLISHNESS, OR PRESUMPTION?

THANK GOD FOR EVERYTHING?

HOW TO BELIEVE GOD FOR A MATE

MARRIAGE AND THE FAMILY
Practical Insight For Family Living

LIVING IN THE REALM OF THE SPIRIT

THE ORIGIN OF SATAN

CONCERNING THEM WHICH ARE ASLEEP

HOMOSEXUALITY:
State of Birth or State of Mind?

PROSPERITY ON GOD'S TERMS

WALKING IN GOD'S WORD
(Through His Promises)

PRACTICAL SUGGESTIONS FOR SUCCESSFUL MINISTRY

NAME IT AND CLAIM IT!
The Power of Positive Confession

THE VICTORIOUS, OVERCOMING LIFE
(A Verse-by-Verse Study of the Book of Colossians)

A NEW LAW FOR A NEW PEOPLE

THE PROMISED LAND
(A New Era for the Body of Christ)

THREE KEYS TO POSITIVE CONFESSION

(continued on next page)

BOOKS BY FREDERICK K.C. PRICE, PH.D.

(continued)

THE WAY, THE WALK,
AND THE WARFARE OF THE BELIEVER
(A Verse-by-Verse Study of the Book of Ephesians)

BEWARE! THE LIES OF SATAN

TESTING THE SPIRITS

THE CHASTENING OF THE LORD

IDENTIFIED WITH CHRIST:
A Complete Cycle From Defeat to Victory

Available from your local bookstore

About the Author

Frederick K. C. Price, Ph.D., founded Crenshaw Christian Center in Los Angeles, California, in 1973, with a congregation of some 300 people. Today, the church's membership numbers well over 14,000 members of various racial backgrounds.

Crenshaw Christian Center, home of the renowned 10,146-seat FaithDome, has a staff of more than 200 employees. Included on its 30-acre grounds are a Ministry Training Institute, the Frederick K.C. Price III elementary, junior, and senior high schools, as well as the FKCP III Child Care Center.

The *Ever Increasing Faith* television and radio broadcasts are outreaches of Crenshaw Christian Center. The television program is viewed on more than 100 stations throughout the United States and overseas. The radio program airs on over 40 stations across the country.

Dr. Price has traveled extensively, teaching the Word of Faith simply and understandably in the power of the Holy Spirit. He is the author of several books on faith and divine healing.

In 1990, Dr. Price founded the Fellowship of Inner-City Word of Faith Ministries (FICWFM) for the purpose of fostering and spreading the faith message among independent ministries located in the urban, metropolitan areas of the United States.